Getting To Know...

Nature's Children

SQUIRRELS

George Peck

PUBLISHER	Joseph R. DeVarennes
PUBLICATION DIRECTOR	Kenneth H. Pearson
MANAGING EDITOR	Valerie Wyatt
SERIES ADVISOR	Merebeth Switzer
SERIES CONSULTANT	Michael Singleton
CONSULTANTS	Ross James
	Kay McKeever
	Dr. Audrey N. Tomera
ADVISORS	Roger Aubin
	Robert Furlonger
	Gaston Lavoie
EDITORIAL SUPERVISOR	Jocelyn Smyth
PRODUCTION MANAGER	Ernest Homewood
PRODUCTION ASSISTANTS	Penelope Moir
	Brock Piper

EDITORS

Katherine Farris	Anne Minguet-Patocka
Sandra Gulland	Sarah Reid
Cristel Kleitsch	Cathy Ripley
Elizabeth MacLeod	Eleanor Tourtel
Pamela Martin	Karin Velcheff

PHOTO EDITORS	Bill Ivy
	Don Markle
DESIGN	Annette Tatchell
CARTOGRAPHER	Jane Davie
PUBLICATION ADMINISTRATION	Kathy Kishimoto
	Monique Lemonnier

ARTISTS

Marianne Collins	Greg Ruhl
Pat Ivy	Mary Theberge

This series is approved and recommended by the Federation of Ontario Naturalists.

DB DB MS

Canadian Cataloguing in Publication Data

Peck, George K.
  Squirrels

(Getting to know—nature's children)
Includes index.
ISBN 0-7172-1912-7

1. Squirrels—Juvenile literature.
I. Title. II. Series.

QL737.R68P42 1985   j599.32'32   C85-098739-3

Have you ever wondered . . .

If you like to collect things and store them away, you have probably been told that you are behaving like a squirrel. Squirrels are famous for their habit of collecting and storing nuts. Besides collecting and storing, squirrels are best known for chattering and scolding and for their amazing treetop acrobatics. They seem to love chasing one another up trees and even leaping from one tree to another, chattering noisily when they stop for breath. And anyone who has seen a dog go after a squirrel knows just how noisy that chattering can get.

No matter where you live—town or country—you probably have squirrel neighbors nearby. Many things squirrels do will be familiar to you. But have you ever wondered:

- where baby squirrels are born?
- where squirrels spend the winter?
- how squirrels can walk along wires or straight down brick walls without falling?

Read on to discover the answers to these and other squirrel questions.

Opposite page:

The Red Squirrel is the smallest tree squirrel in North America.

Almost Ready—
But Not Quite

Within days these young squirrels will be scampering through the branches and fending for themselves. Right now their home in the tree seems snug and safe, while the outside world looks big and rather scary.

Adult tree squirrels are bold and curious, but very young squirrels are quite timid. They are likely to run for cover at the slightest hint of anything strange or dangerous. These young ones have probably not gone very far from the nest yet, but they are getting bigger and braver day by day. Soon their curiosity will overcome their nervousness and they will be ready to face the world on their own.

"Maybe tomorrow . . ."
(Gray Squirrel)

6

Meet the Relatives

The squirrel family is a large one. There are about 50 different kinds of squirrels. And squirrels of one kind or another are found almost everywhere in the world, except in the desert areas of Egypt and Arabia and in southerly areas such as Australia, New Zealand and the tip of South America.

In North America, there are squirrels that live mainly in trees and squirrels that live in burrows in the ground. The burrow-living squirrels include Prairie Dogs, marmots, woodchucks, chipmunks and Ground Squirrels. The tree squirrels include the Gray Squirrel, Fox Squirrel, Flying Squirrel and the Red Squirrel. The tree squirrels that most North Americans know best are the Gray Squirrel and the Red Squirrel.

A Gray Squirrel is perfectly at home in city yards and parks.

Where Gray Squirrels live in North America.

Opposite page:

Heading down. (Red Squirrel)

Squirrels Everywhere

Gray Squirrels are found mainly in southern Canada and the eastern United States. Many Gray Squirrels are city dwellers. One reason for this is that cities are safe places to live because few squirrel enemies live there.

Cities are also good places for squirrels to find handouts. Lots of people supply them with tidbits, some willingly—others unwillingly. Almost anyone who puts out seeds for the birds has watched squirrels gobble them all up. To discourage these food snatchers, many bird feeders are equipped with metal collars designed to keep squirrels from climbing up. Even so, bird feeders are still a good source of food for squirrels. Birds scatter seed on the ground as they feed and squirrels are quick to clean up after them.

Red Squirrels are found all across Canada and in several parts of the United States. They will live almost anywhere there are forests, but unlike Gray Squirrels, they are seldom seen in towns and cities. They are not very neighborly and prefer to live alone in the wild.

Squirrel Territory

Gray Squirrels spend most of their time in their home range. The female's range may be two to six hectares (5-15 acres); the male's is larger, sometimes as big as 20 hectares (50 acres). Gray Squirrels are quite happy to share their home range with other squirrels and birds.

Red Squirrels, on the other hand, are much more exclusive. Once it has claimed a territory as its home base, a Red Squirrel will usually chase or frighten away anything that it considers a trespasser. Trespassers might include crows and jays, as well as other squirrels. A Red Squirrel's territory is usually about three-quarters of a hectare (2 acres), but it might be larger or smaller depending on how much food is available.

Where Red Squirrels live in North America.

Pictures never lie. Here is a black Gray Squirrel with a red tail!

Squirrel Chatter

Next time you take a quiet walk in the woods, listen for the sound of squirrels talking.

If a Red Squirrel is puzzled, it sometimes makes a soft *whuck whuck* sound. But you are more likely to hear a loud, rough *tcherr tcherr*. This is the Red Squirrel's scolding call. If you can see the squirrel, you will probably find that it is stamping its feet and jerking its tail as it calls. The message is clear: "Get out of my territory."

Gray Squirrels have similar calls that they make when they are threatened or annoyed, and they also flick their tails to signal their moods.

Calling for mom.

Squirrels Up Close

Red Squirrels have a reddish-brown coat with a white underside and a white ring around their eyes. In the summer, a black stripe on both sides of the squirrel's body separates the red from the white underside. In winter, the Red Squirrel's coat is darker and thicker, and there is no side stripe. Instead a single orangey-red stripe runs down the middle of its back.

Not all Gray Squirrels are gray. Some are black or even a reddish color. Since Gray Squirrels are quite a bit bigger than Red Squirrels, it is unlikely that you would mistake a reddish Gray Squirrel for a Red Squirrel.

An adult Gray Squirrel is usually about 50 centimetres (20 inches) long from the tip of its nose to the end of its bushy tail. Red Squirrels are generally a little more than half as long when fully grown.

Size Comparison

Gray Squirrel

Red Squirrel

Opposite page:

Can you tell if this Red Squirrel is wearing its summer or its winter coat?

Summer and Winter Coats

Do you have winter and summer jackets? If you do, you have something in common with in squirrels. In the summer they have a lightweight coat, so that they do not get too hot. In fall they grow a thicker winter coat.

A squirrel's coat is actually two coats in one. A thick short undercoat traps in body heat, while longer guard hairs shed water and snow. In winter, even the soles of a squirrel's feet grow fur. This not only helps keep the squirrel warm, but also gives it a better grip on wet or icy branches.

Dressed for winter.
(Gray Squirrel)

Treetop Acrobats

Circus acrobats must envy squirrels. These furry athletes are as much at home in the trees as we are on the ground. They use their strong, sharp claws to dig into the rough bark. This makes them so surefooted that they can climb down trees headfirst and even climb up brick walls. Squirrels can often travel quite far without ever touching the ground by leaping from tree to tree. As they leap from one branch to the other, their tails act as rudders and help them balance.

If squirrels want to get to the ground quickly, they simply jump. By spreading their legs and holding their tails out they can glide just enough to break their fall. Red Squirrels have jumped or fallen from branches 36 metres (120 feet) above the ground without being hurt. Jumps of about nine metres (30 feet) are normal.

This young Gray Squirrel is learning that practice makes perfect.

Life on the Ground

Sharp claws and a rudderlike tail are not the squirrel's only acrobatic equipment. It also has excellent eyesight. This helps the squirrel know exactly how far to leap to get to the next branch.

Even though squirrels spend much of their time in the trees, they often come down to the ground to look for food and to store it, or to get to another tree that is too far away to reach by jumping. They usually walk slowly when feeding on the ground, but if danger threatens, they can bound to the nearest tree and scamper up to safety in no time.

You'll never find a squirrel too far from a tree.

Watch Out!

Squirrels have to be constantly alert as there are many animals that see them as a tasty meal. They must be on the lookout for coyotes, foxes, skunks, raccoons, wolves, lynx, bobcats, and some kinds of hawks and owls, among others. But a squirrel's most dangerous enemies are some kinds of weasels. These agile animals can climb trees and are almost as surefooted as squirrels are.

To escape from weasels and other tree-climbing enemies, squirrels must move very fast or find a small space to duck into. Most squirrels soon get to know every nook and cranny in their range. They know where all the best hiding places are, and are lightning-quick to scoot into one of them when chased.

Something up there must be pretty interesting—and what better place to watch from than a tree-hole you can duck back into in a flash!

Tree Houses

Many squirrels make their home high up in the trees. In winter, and when they are raising a family, they usually den in a hole in a tree. It may be a natural hole, or the squirrel may take over a deserted woodpecker home. In summer, or if no holes are available, squirrels often build large nests of twigs and leaves. These nests are called dreys.

If you saw a drey, you might mistake it for a shaggy pile of leaves and twigs that have got caught in the crotch of a tree. Actually it is a carefully woven waterproof house, with a small entranceway that leads into a round snug room lined with pine needles.

Some Red Squirrels spend winters in ground dens, in a fallen tree, rockpile or under tree roots. They build tree nests—or take over abandoned crow or hawk nests—in summer.

Red Squirrels usually live alone, but will sometimes share a nest or den with their young for a winter. Gray Squirrels are more sociable; sometimes as many as six Grays will cuddle up together in a drey.

This is a squirrel's drey.

Opposite page:

It's business as usual in winter except on the bitterest days.

26

Clean, But Messy

Squirrels are very careful to keep their coats clean. They spend a lot of time licking their fur and grooming it with their paws. This is important because clean and fluffy hair insulates the squirrel from hot and cold by trapping a layer of air against its skin.

But while squirrels keep themselves very clean, they are bad housekeepers. When their nests or dens get littered with twigs, leaves and dirt, they simply move on instead of cleaning up. Imagine what would happen if your family never bothered to take its garbage out. You would probably have to move often too.

Fair-Weather Days

In spring, summer and fall, a squirrel's day starts at sunrise. Depending on what needs to be done, the squirrel spends the first few hours of the day bustling around getting itself a meal, gathering and storing food or gathering nesting materials.

By mid-day the squirrel is ready for a rest. And what better way to relax than to bask in the sun or curl up in one's nest for an afternoon nap? Towards the end of the day, the squirrel may go out again in search of food. Both Gray Squirrels and Red Squirrels are most active during the day, but they are occasionally seen out looking for a snack on a moonlit summer night.

Lolling in the sun.

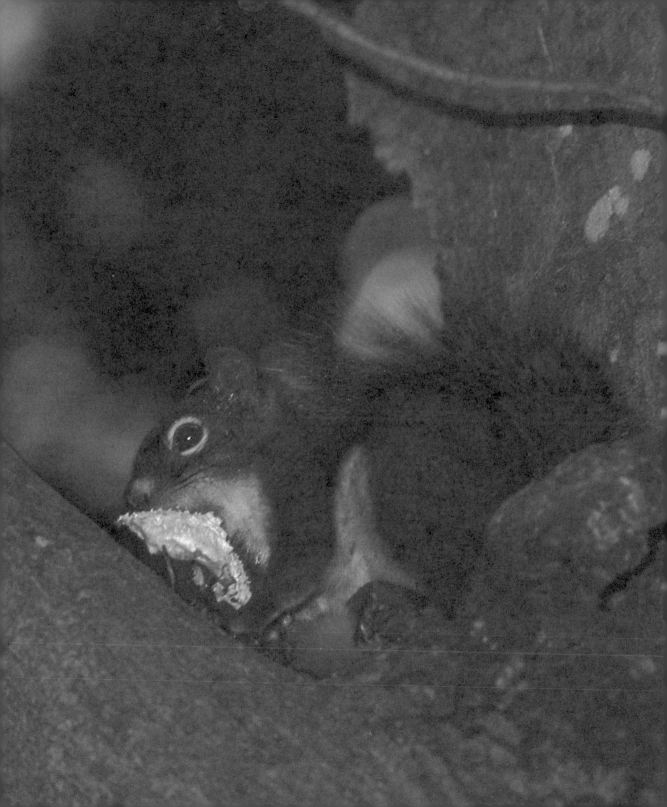

A Varied Menu

Did you know that squirrels help plant our forests? They collect nuts and store them in shallow holes dug in the ground. Some nuts are dug up again later and eaten. But squirrels bury so many nuts that they never find them all again. The lost nuts often take root, and, in time, grow into new trees.

While squirrels have a definite passion for nuts, they eat many other kinds of food as well, including buds, flowers, seeds, berries, fruit and mushrooms. Most squirrels will also eat insects, grubs and birds' eggs if they come across them.

Red Squirrels are somewhat more enthusiastic about meat than other squirrels. They will occasionally dine on snails, small birds, mice and even young rabbits. They will also gnaw on old bones or antlers they find on the forest floor. The Red Squirrel's wide-ranging appetite helps to explain why it is found in so many different parts of North America. It can get itself a meal just about anywhere.

Opposite page:

Red Squirrels are very fond of mushrooms. They will even eat those that are deadly to us, with no ill effects!

A Built-In Nutcracker

Squirrels, like all rodents, have two pairs of large, sharp front teeth called incisors. These teeth never stop growing, but they are worn down and sharpened against each other as the squirrel uses them.

With these powerful teeth, squirrels can quickly and easily crack open the hardest nut to get at the tasty meat or kernel inside. The squirrel holds the nut between its nimble front paws, often turning it around as it removes the tough outer husk.

Next time you pass under an oak or walnut tree in the fall, look carefully at the ground beneath it. You might see bits of shells and husks that will tell you that a squirrel has recently been feasting in the branches above you.

Brrr! It's Cold Outside

Tree squirrels, unlike some of their burrow-dwelling cousins, do not hibernate during the winter. Instead, they remain active, only staying in their dens during severe storms and blizzards. In Alaska, Red Squirrels have been seen outside on days when the temperature has fallen as low as –34 degrees Celsius (–30 degrees Fahrenheit).

Because food is scarce in the winter, squirrels must gather and store food in the fall. They do this by instinct, that is, they do it without thinking about it or planning it.

Squirrels store food in different ways, depending on the food. Hard nuts are stored singly in shallow holes in the ground. The cones of pine and other trees are stored in heaps above ground. One heap may contain hundreds of cones. Soft foods, such as fruit or mushrooms, are stored in forks of trees to dry out, so that they will last until they are needed.

Opposite page:

Squirrels rely heavily on their keen sense of smell to find food under the snow since they soon forget where they have buried it.

Starting a Family

Gray Squirrels mate in January, while Red Squirrels mate in February and March. Both kinds of squirrels sometimes mate again in the summer. Mating season is a time of great excitement. A number of male squirrels will chase a female who has signalled that she is ready to mate. These chases often last for quite a long time and are accompanied by much chattering and tail-twitching. There are seldom serious fights among the males, but there is a lot of scolding and some pushing, until one of the males is chosen by the female as her mate.

Usually the male leaves after mating, but sometimes the pair will stay together for a while and even build a nest together. But the male is always gone by the time the babies arrive.

"Which way did he go?"

Tiny Babies

After mating, the female prepares a home for her babies. She prefers the comfort and safety of a tree den, but if no tree holes are available, she will build a drey. In either case, she will pay particular attention to furnishing her nursery. It will be well lined with strips of bark and leaves to make a soft warm place for the babies.

About a month and a half after mating, the mother squirrel gives birth to her babies. A Red Squirrel mother usually has three to five young, although she may have fewer or as many as eight. Gray Squirrel families are usually slightly smaller.

The baby squirrels are born tiny, pink and naked. Their eyes and ears are sealed shut, and they have no teeth. Red Squirrel newborns are about 70 millimetres (3 inches) long and weigh less than seven grams (a quarter of an ounce). Newborn Gray Squirrels are about twice this size.

Opposite page:

These newborn Red Squirrels must wait almost a month before their eyes open.

A Devoted Mother

The mother squirrel spends a great deal of time with her babies in the first weeks of their lives. This is a private time for the mother squirrel and her family. She chases all intruders away from her den or nest and the area around it. Even the father squirrel is not allowed in.

If the privacy of her den or nest is threatened, a mother squirrel will sometimes move her young to a new home. To do this she carries them, one by one, in her mouth, like a cat carries her kittens. If she meets an animal that she sees as a threat while she is carrying a baby, she will set the baby down for a moment and bravely drive off the intruder.

These eager young Gray Squirrels can hardly wait to explore the world outside their den.

Fast-Growing Babies

By the time they are three weeks old, baby squirrels have their two bottom front teeth, and some hair on their backs. Their ears open by four weeks of age, and their eyes are open by the time they are five weeks old. At first their eyes are a cloudy blue color, but they gradually clear until they are bright and black, and the young squirrels can see properly.

During these first weeks, baby squirrels nurse on their mother's rich milk. This helps them grow quickly. By seven weeks, the young squirrels start to eat some solid food. By the time that they are 10 to 12 weeks of age, the babies no longer nurse at all. Instead they eat the same kinds of food their mother eats.

"Make room for me!"
(Red Squirrel)

Making It On Their Own

The young squirrels are ready to look after themselves by the time they stop nursing. They will now leave their cozy den and begin a full, active life in the trees. In the late summer, many young squirrels start building their own leaf nests in the crotches of trees. At first their shelters are small and loosely made, but gradually they learn how to build better ones.

In the fall the young squirrels start preparing for winter just like their parents. They collect and store a supply of food, and they may look for a good spot for a winter den. Not all young squirrels leave their mother before their first winter. Some will stay with her and share her winter home.

When spring comes again, the young squirrels are ready to start their own families, in their own homes. Most squirrels only live to be about five years old, but some live three times that long and have many families over the years.

Special Words

Burrow   A hole dug in the ground by an animal for use as a home.

Den   Animal home.

Drey   A leaf nest built by squirrels.

Guard hairs   Long coarse hairs that make up the outer layer of the squirrel's coat.

Hibernate   To go into a heavy sleep for the winter.

Incisors   Front teeth used for cutting or gnawing.

Litter   Young animals born together.

Mate   To come together to produce young. Either member of an animal pair is also the other's mate.

Nurse   To drink milk from the mother's body.

Rodent   An animal with a certain kind of teeth, which are especially good for gnawing.

Territory   Area that an animal or group of animals lives in and defends from other animals of the same kind.

INDEX

Cover Photo: Bill Ivy

Photo Credits: Wayne Lankinen (Valan Photos), pages 4, 40; Bill Ivy, pages 7, 8, 12, 15, 19, 20, 23, 24, 27, 28, 31, 32, 35, 36, 39, 43, 44; Bill Ivy (Miller Services), page 11; Stephen J. Krasemann (Valan Photos), page 16.

Getting To Know...

Nature's Children

FROGS

Bill Ivy

PUBLISHER	Joseph R. DeVarennes
PUBLICATION DIRECTOR	Kenneth H. Pearson
MANAGING EDITOR	Valerie Wyatt
SERIES ADVISOR	Merebeth Switzer
SERIES CONSULTANT	Michael Singleton
CONSULTANTS	Ross James
	Kay McKeever
	Dr. Audrey N. Tomera
ADVISORS	Roger Aubin
	Robert Furlonger
	Gaston Lavoie
EDITORIAL SUPERVISOR	Jocelyn Smyth
PRODUCTION MANAGER	Ernest Homewood
PRODUCTION ASSISTANTS	Penelope Moir
	Brock Piper

EDITORS

Katherine Farris   Anne Minguet-Patocka
Sandra Gulland   Sarah Reid
Cristel Kleitsch   Cathy Ripley
Elizabeth MacLeod   Eleanor Tourtel
Pamela Martin   Karin Velcheff

PHOTO EDITORS	Bill Ivy
	Don Markle
DESIGN	Annette Tatchell
CARTOGRAPHER	Jane Davie
PUBLICATION ADMINISTRATION	Kathy Kishimoto
	Monique Lemonnier

ARTISTS

Marianne Collins   Greg Ruhl
Pat Ivy   Mary Theberge

This series is approved and recommended
by the Federation of Ontario Naturalists.

Canadian Cataloguing in Publication Data

Ivy, Bill, 1953-
  Frogs

(Getting to know—nature's children)
Includes index.
ISBN 0-7172-1916-X

1. Frogs—Juvenile literature.
I. Title.   II. Series.

QL668.E2I97 1985   j597.8'9   C85-098713-X

Have you ever wondered . . .

You probably know what a frog looks like. Throughout the world, fairy tales tell of the handsome prince who has been turned into a frog and can only be changed back again by a kiss. In real life few people are willing to kiss a frog. Perhaps that is because many still believe that a frog will give them warts. That simply is not true. You cannot get warts from a frog or from a toad.

Sitting hunched on a lily pad with its bulging eyes and wide mouth, the frog appears lost in thought. Is it pondering some serious question? Or is it just thinking about dinner? As you will see, a frog should have lots to think about. Its life is one of the most interesting in all of nature. It starts out as an egg that hatches into a tadpole that lives in water and then changes into a completely different creature that can walk on land! Both above and below the water, its days are full of adventure and danger.

Let's take a look at a frog's life and find out if the well-known Muppet Kermit is right when he says, "It's not easy being green!"

Opposite page:

Bullfrog.

Overleaf:

The Leopard Frog searches moist grassy meadows for food.

Where They Live

The frog is a very unusual animal. Like the toad and salamander it is an amphibian, which is a Greek word meaning "two lives." Indeed the frog does live two lives, one as a water animal and one as a land animal.

There are 2600 different kinds of frogs in the world. About 100 of these live in North America. Frogs of one type or another can be found in every American state and most of Canada. There is a kind of frog for almost every kind of habitat. Some, such as Bullfrogs, live in big lakes. Others prefer marshes or meadows. Still others, the tree frogs, live in trees. But no matter where they live as adults, all frogs start life in water.

The Green Tree Frog is considered by many to be the most beautiful of all tree frogs. It makes its home in the southern United States.

Survival Skin

If you have ever held a frog, you probably noticed how cold and clammy it felt. A frog's skin is very different from yours. For one thing, a frog can "breathe" through it. That's right, a frog gets some of the oxygen its body needs (and sometimes all of it) through its skin. Because of this, the frog's blood vessels must be very near the surface of its body. It cannot afford to have several layers of dry skin covering its body as you do. Instead, it has a moist, thin skin so that oxygen can pass through it to the blood vessels.

As a frog grows, its skin becomes tighter and tighter. In time it literally grows too big for its skin! When the skin can stretch no more, it splits apart into patches which gradually fall off. Fortunately for the frog, a new layer of skin has grown in under the old. Not one to waste food, the newly dressed frog eats its old coat for dinner!

Opposite page:

The Gray Tree Frog is a master of the art of camouflage. It can quickly change its color to match its surroundings.

Leap Frog, Anyone?

A frog's body is ideal for life both in and out of the water. Thanks to its powerful back legs, it is an excellent jumper and swimmer. Frogs seldom walk. They prefer to hop. Some species can leap an amazing 20 times their own body length. That is like you long-jumping a football field!

In the water, frogs are equally at home. Each back foot has five toes with a thin web of skin betwen them. Using their feet as paddles to do the frog kick, these champion swimmers glide effortlessly through the water. In fact, the design of the frog's foot is so perfect that deep diving flippers are patterned after it. Now you know why skin divers are called frogmen!

Can you guess where this Leopard Frog got its name? Of course—from its spots!

A Frog's Eye View

The frog's large bulging eyes give it an almost comical look. Imagine how silly you would look with eyes like those! But to a frog they have many advantages.

In order for you to see properly, both of your eyes must focus together on the same thing. Believe it or not, at any one time, both of the frog's eyes are looking in opposite directions. This means that even though it cannot turn its head, it can see around itself in almost a complete circle! No wonder it is so difficult to catch a frog by surprise!

Unlike you, a frog does not close its eyes by moving its eyelids. It moves its eyes! It pulls them into their sockets, and this allows its eyelids to close. A frog also has an extra eyelid which is transparent and blinks up from the bottom to keep its eyes clean and moist. Underwater, this clear window protects the eyes and acts as the frog's diving mask.

A frog's eyes even act as a periscope. They poke up above the water when the rest of the frog's body lies under the surface.

Opposite page:

Although the Bullfrog is North America's largest frog, its name refers to its bellowing call and not its size.

Gulp!

A frog's menu is simple—if something moves, eat it! Anything small enough to fit into a frog's mouth may be sampled. Crayfish, snails, slugs, worms, fish and insects of all kinds are potential meals if they come too close.

Frogs have terrible table manners. They do not chew their food politely. Instead they swallow it whole in one great big gulp. Larger prey are stuffed into their mouths with both hands, and then tiny teeth on the upper jaw stop the meal from escaping. Incredibly, to help get its food down, the frog even pulls its eyes way into their sockets and uses them to help shove the food down its throat. Its eyes actually drop into its head and pop out again!

With many frogs it is easy to tell a male from a female: the male's eardrums are larger than his eyes.

Sharp Shooter!

When catching small insects, the frog shows a little more class. Sitting very still, it patiently waits for dinner to arrive. When an insect comes within range, the frog attacks. Shooting out its long sticky tongue, it strikes the startled creature. Immediately the tongue is flipped back into the mouth with the frog's next meal stuck to its tip. All this happens so fast you can hardly see it! The frog is an excellent marksman and does not miss its target very often. It can even pick a fly right out of the air!

Opposite page:

On the lookout.
(Spring Peeper)

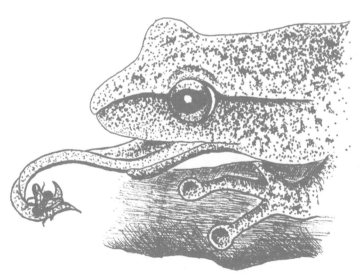

Great Escapes

A frog's life is not all fun and games and eating insects. It has to avoid being eaten too. It is always on the alert for enemies, such as a hungry heron, otter, weasel, owl, skunk, fox or fish. But its most deadly enemy is the Garter Snake. A Garter Snake will gladly dine on frog at any meal.

To protect itself, the frog relies on its keen eyesight and sharp hearing. When on shore it always sits facing the water. On each side of its head are two large, round eardrums that are very sensitive to sound. At the slightest crack of a twig or at the first sign of danger, the frog dives in and swims to the bottom of the pond. Its slippery skin makes it as tricky to grab as a bar of soap in a tub.

When captured, the Mink Frog emits a scent which resembles that of a mink.

Still many frogs are caught. Some scream for their lives when captured. Often this sudden noise startles their enemy long enough for them to escape. Others swallow air and puff themselves up, hoping to convince their attackers they are too big to swallow.

In addition frogs rely on camouflage. This means that they are colored and patterned to blend in with their surroundings, so that they are difficult to see. Some frogs, such as tree frogs, can even change color to suit their surroundings. Blending in with their surroundings helps frogs avoid the many hungry eyes constantly on the lookout for food.

You can recognize a Wood Frog by its dark bandit's mask.

Look Up!

Tree frog feet

Front

Hind

If you have ever gone hunting for frogs, you have probably searched the water's edge and tall grasses. The next time you go frog hunting, look up. You just might see a tree frog.

While most frogs live on the ground, these expert gymnasts leave the water after mating and egg-laying to climb up trees and shrubs. Using tiny suction cups on the tip of their toes, they can scale almost any surface.

Of the 13 kinds of tree frogs found in North America, most are shorter than a stick of gum and light enough to stand on a leaf. They are all excellent musicians and love to sing just before a thunderstorm. Their color can vary from hour to hour depending on the temperature and light, and so they are hard to see. If you hear a high trill on a hot summer's night, it could be one of these tiny frog minstrels announcing its presence. Remember, look up!

Hang in there! (Gray Tree Frog)

Minstrels of the Pond

In spring, most frogs gather in ponds or marshes to mate and lay their eggs. Some types of frogs head for water early in the spring, when there is still ice. Others, such as the Bullfrog, wait for warmer weather—and warmer water—later in the spring.

When they get to their pond or marsh, the males begin to sing loudly, in some cases to announce their territory but more often to impress a female with their songs, Each species has its own distinct call. One frog barks like a dog, another sounds like a man snoring. Others whistle, chirp or trill like birds.

The most welcome of all the calls is that of the Spring Peeper. Its high clear preep-preep-preep is the first song we hear after the long winter. When heard from a distance, a chorus of peepers sounds like sleigh bells. But the most familiar frog voice of all belongs to the deep-voiced Bullfrog. Its loud "jug-o-rum" call echoes like a foghorn and can be heard almost a kilometre (half a mile) away!

Opposite page:

Because it is so small, the Spring Peeper is more often heard than seen.

Singing with its Mouth Closed

Have you ever wondered how a frog makes its croaks, preeps or chirps? Believe it or not, it actually sings with its mouth and nostrils closed! After taking a deep breath, the frog pumps the air back and forth through its voice box and into a sac in the throat or on the sides of its head. In some species, this vocal sac inflates to an enormous size—almost as big as the frog itself! To watch a frog sing you might think it is actually blowing bubble gum balloons!

Surprisingly, most female frogs have very weak voices or none at all. They are simply the audience to which all the song is directed. You might think that female frogs would respond to any male, however, that is not true. They only react to the mating call of males of their own species.

The Western Chorus Frog makes its home in clearings and open fields.

Eggs Galore

In the spring or early summer, the female frog deposits her eggs in the water, and the male covers them with sperm, a substance that starts them developing into tadpoles. Anywhere from 100 to 20 000 eggs are laid, depending on the type of frog.

Unlike bird eggs, frog eggs do not have hard shells. Instead, each one is protected by a thick layer of clear jelly that swells up in the water. The jelly also holds the eggs together. This slippery mass of tiny dark eggs is known as frog spawn. If you were to try and scoop some spawn out of the water, it would simply slide right through your fingers.

The tiny tadpoles growing inside the eggs get their nourishment from their jelly covering. Some types are ready to hatch in a few days, others take a week or more.

Wood Frog with eggs.

Hatch Day

Escaping from the jelly could be a problem for the tadpole. But luckily, by the time it has developed, the spawn has thinned out. Wriggling its little tail, the tiny tadpole swims free and attaches itself to a plant using a sucker under its head.

What a strange creature this newborn is! It is not completely developed. Its head and body are all one, and it has no eyes or mouth. A featherlike gill on each side of the head enables it to breathe underwater.

Soon, as if by magic, eyes develop and the tadpole sees the world for the very first time. Now its outside gills disappear and are replaced by new ones under the skin. A small, round mouth also forms, equipped with a parrotlike beak and sharp teeth. This is the perfect tool for eating tiny water plants and animals or for scraping algae off rocks.

The tadpole has an enormous appetite and almost doubles in size within a few days. At the same time, it is secreting a film of slime over its body to become more streamlined and help ward off disease.

Opposite page:

The jelly surrounding these eggs provides warmth for the developing tadpoles. It is also bitter to the taste, which discourages predators.

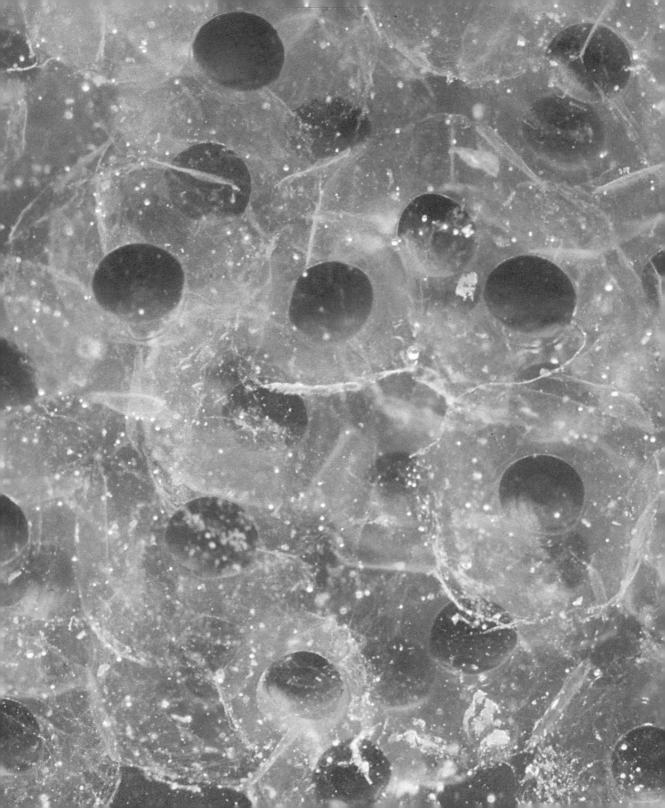

Peculiar Predators

Life is hazardous for the little tadpole. It has many enemies. Fish, turtles, water bugs and birds all enjoy a tasty tadpole meal. Sometimes a Wolf Spider will run aross the water and seize an unsuspecting tadpole and drag it to shore to be eaten later. But the strangest enemy of all is the bladderwort—a plant that actually eats tadpoles.

This bizarre plant floats in the water and has small sacs along the edge of its leaves. Each of these sacs has bristles along its edge and a trapdoor that opens from the bottom. If a careless tadpole swims too close and rubs against the hairs, the trapdoor quickly opens, sucks in the surprised victim and slams shut. Poor tadpole! There is no hope for escape from the bladderwort.

Green Frog tadpole.

Frogs Forever

A tadpole's best defense against its predators is to stay as still as possible and not draw attention to itself. However, very few survive.

This is not as bad as it sounds if you remember how many eggs a mother frog lays. Although some of the eggs get gobbled up by leeches, beetles and other insects, a great many are left to develop into tadpoles. In fact, if only half the tadpoles lived to be adults, we would be overrun with frogs! As things are, it is estimated that for every 20 eggs laid one will survive to become a frog.

Unlike frogs, toads are covered in warts. Their skin is drier and they are fatter and heavier. Can you tell if this singing minstrel is a frog or a toad? (American Toad)

The Great Change

As the tadpole grows it starts to eat more animals than plants. Small water creatures become part of its diet.

Inside the tadpole's body, many changes are taking place. These changes are as incredible as those that occur inside a moth's cocoon.

Gradually the tadpole's gills change into air-breathing lungs and it begins to surface for air. Back legs begin to grow—first one, then the other breaks through the skin. Next, front legs sprout, and the tadpole's mouth widens and its eyes bulge. Before too long the hind legs are large enough to help with swimming.

If the changing tadpole loses one of its limbs, all is not lost—a new one will grow in its place! This is only true for this stage of its life. When it is an adult frog, it will not be able to replace a leg. As each day passes, the tadpole looks more and more like its parents.

Still a tadpole, but looking more like a frog every day. (Green Frog)

Tadpole or Frog?

When all four legs are fully grown, the tadpole is caught between two worlds. Is it a frog with a tail or a tadpole with legs? What do you think?

Before it is ready to hop out of the water as a mature, adult frog, one more change must take place. This curious in-between creature stops eating and lives off the food stored in its tail. This "tail food" is slowly absorbed into its body. Once the tail has almost disappeared, there is no more doubt—the tadpole has become a frog!

For most types of frogs, the whole process from egg to frog takes about two months. But for others, a much longer time is needed. The Bullfrog, for example, takes a long two years to complete the cycle.

A Green Frog ventures out of the water for the first time.

A New Beginning

The new frog must now learn how to hop on dry land. It is a little clumsy at first, but soon it is as comfortable on shore as it is in the water. A new chapter in its life has begun.

There are other skills to master, and the new frog masters them quickly. It soon becomes adept at catching food and learns to be alert in order to avoid being dinner for somebody else. It spends the hot summer days immersed in the cool water of the pond. Its big eyes watch all the comings and goings around it.

Then the air and water start turning colder. Soon colored leaves are falling into the water. Winter is on its way.

By absorbing oxygen from the water through its skin, a frog can stay underwater for a long time. (Leopard Frog)

The Deep Sleep

Frogs, like all amphibians, are cold-blooded. This means their bodies cannot control their temperature as yours can. A frog's body temperature rises and falls with the outside temperature. If a frog gets too hot or cold, it will die. But what happens to frogs in cold-weather country when winter comes? How do they survive the freezing temperatures?

Like many animals, they go into a deep sleep called hibernation. Some burrow into the ground, others simply choose a sheltered spot under a log or stone. But most dig themselves into the muddy bottom of a pond or lake. There they stop breathing through their lungs and absorb oxygen from the water through

their skin. A hibernating frog's heartbeat slows down greatly, and it will not eat or move a muscle until the following spring.

Eventually the warm weather returns, and this modern day Rip Van Winkle climbs out to greet the world with frog song. And the miraculous cycle of change from egg to tadpole to frog starts all over again.

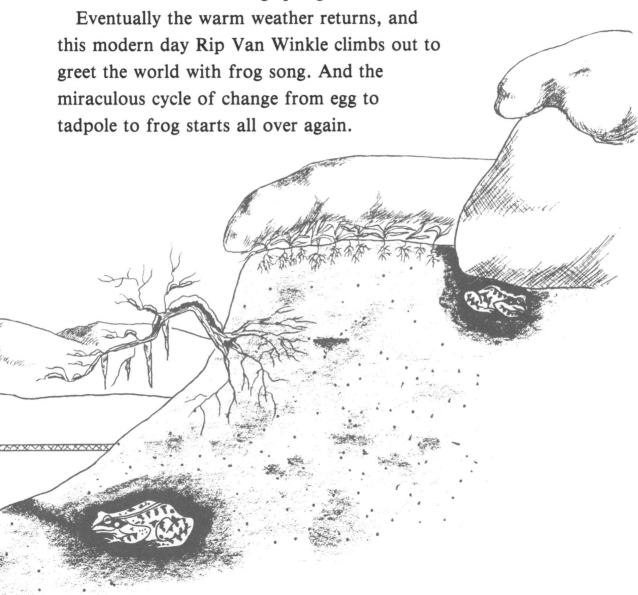

Frogs and Us

For centuries frogs have fascinated both children and adults alike. The frog's incredible transformation is easily observed and is still one of the great wonders of life.

Frogs are not just interesting, they are also helpful. They help us by eating large numbers of harmful insects. In fact many gardeners keep them in ponds for this very reason. So the next time you see a frog, be sure to stop and say thanks to this remarkable little animal for all the help and the pleasure it gives us.

Special Words

Algae   Very simple water plants that often form a scum on rocks.

Amphibians   A group of animals that live both on land and in water. Frogs, toads, newts and salamanders are amphibians.

Blood vessels   Tubes, arteries and veins through which blood flows in the body.

Camouflage   Colors and patterns that help an animal blend in with its surroundings.

Gills   Openings on a tadpole's head that take in water and extract the oxygen in it.

Habitat   The area or type of area in which an animal or plant naturally lives.

Hibernation   A sleeplike state that lasts all winter long.

Lungs   Parts of the body that extract oxygen from the air so that it can be used by the body.

Oxygen   The part of the air that most living things need in order to survive.

Sperm   A substance made in the male's body that is needed to start new life.

Spawn   A mass of frog eggs held together by a jelly-like substance.

Tadpole   The name for a frog hatchling.

INDEX